A Young Dancer's Apprenticeship

ON TOUR WITH THE MOSCOW CITY BALLET

A Young Dancer's Apprenticeship

by OLYMPIA DOWD

Twenty-First Century Books
Brookfield, Connecticut

Copyright © 2003 by Olympia Dowd

Photographs copyright © 2003 by John Dowd.

Published in 2003 by Twenty-First Century Books
A Division of The Millbrook Press, Inc.
2 Old New Milford Road
Brookfield, Connecticut 06804
www.millbrookpress.com

First published in Canada in 2002 by Raincoast Books
9050 Shaughnessy Street
Vancouver, British Columbia
V6P 6E5
www.raincoast.com

Performance and rehearsal photos from Russia, Asia and the United Kingdom
are printed with permission of Moscow City Ballet (The Theatre of
Classical Ballet of Smirnov-Golovanov).

LIBRARY OF CONGRESS CATALOGING-IN-PUBLICATION DATA
Dowd, Olympia, 1984–
A young dancer's apprenticeship : on tour with
the Moscow City Ballet / Olympia Dowd.
p. cm.
Includes index.
Summary: An autobiography of a Canadian ballet student who, while still in her early teens,
was offered the chance to study and tour with the Moscow City Ballet.
ISBN 0-7613-2917-X (lib. bdg.) 0-7613-1898-4 (pbk.)
1. Dowd, Olympia, 1984—Juvenile literature.
2. Ballet dancers—British Columbia—Vancouver—Biography—Juvenile literature.
3. Moscow City Ballet—Juvenile literature.
[1. Dowd, Olympia, 1984–
2. Ballet dancers. 3. Moscow City Ballet. 4. Women—Biography.
5. Youths' writings.] I. Title.
GV1785.D665 A3 2003
792.8'028'092—DC21

2002008282

Printed in Hong Kong
5 4 3 2 1

Contents

Part 1

Surprise Audition in Vancouver

THERE WAS NOTHING special about that warm June morning to suggest events that would turn my life upside down. Tipped off by a small notice in a dance newsletter, I had come to the Russian Community Centre for the start of a five-day Vaganova ballet workshop—something to fill the gap between the end of the ballet year and the start of summer school.

Inside the dark, old building on Fourth Avenue in Vancouver were two men and a woman who spoke Russian. One man introduced himself as Ian Robertson, the event's organizer. He was from town, but the man and woman with him were from Moscow. The woman had short, shiny black hair, a very dramatic face and big green eyes. The man had a mustache and gray hair and wore glasses. All three scrutinized each of the dancers murmuring to each other as we came in to the studio to stretch.

OPPOSITE PAGE
Reaching for excellence.

The polished wooden floor was slippery but fortunately I had a bag of resin with me (I had vowed never to be without one after a recent experience dancing *en pointe* on a particularly bad stage).

The woman gave a very good, very hard class. The man with the glasses worked the cassette-player but watched everything very carefully. At the end of class Mr. Robertson took me aside. Translating for the Russians, who were earlier introduced as the artistic director and ballet mistress of Moscow City Ballet, he told me that they would like to use me in their company's first North American tour in 18 months' time. I would be part of a Vancouver-based cast hired for *The Nutcracker* and other, future productions. I could scarcely believe my ears.

At home I pored over the information my mother had picked up from the registration desk before class. Moscow City Ballet was a touring company with some fifty dancers and a strong focus on the classical repertoire. The man with the glasses was Artistic Director Victor Smirnov-Golovanov —trained at the Moscow Choreographic Institute, twenty years a soloist with the Bolshoi Ballet, nineteen years the artistic director of the Odessa Ballet Theatre, and founder of the Moscow City Ballet (MCB) in 1989. The beautiful, intense woman was Ludmila Nerubashenko, head ballet mistress at MCB for the past six years. She had been a soloist with the Odessa Ballet and a principal with MCB.

I could barely wait for the next day. Before class, Mr. Robertson asked if I'd ever considered moving to Moscow. "Funny, I can't say that's ever crossed my mind," I quipped, thinking he was joking. He wasn't. "Here's what's happening: Instead of waiting until the ballet tours North America next year, they want you to join the company in Moscow right away," he said. "And they would like to train you as the Lilac Fairy" (a major role in *Sleeping Beauty)*. "Do they know I'm only 14?" I asked him. "They know," he responded, smiling.

My parents were understandably surprised at the turn of events. "Who are these people, some kind of a pedophile ring?" my father asked. Before anything further could happen, he rang Irina Carlsen-Reid for advice. A retired professor of Slavonic Studies, Irina had studied ballet in her youth and had many contacts in Moscow and St. Petersburg. We had met at my dance school where she had taught Ballet History, designed several large

One of my early Carmen poses.

productions, and acted as interpreter for the Russian guest teachers the school occasionally brought in to help with repertoire coaching or summer school. She quickly telephoned her friend Natalia Zolotova, a *grande dame* of ballet in Moscow, to ask what she knew about the company. Madame Zolotova's answer was that MCB was reputable, one of several privately run Moscow troupes that toured internationally (from Hong Kong to the United Kingdom, from Israel to Japan and the Philippines). She knew Victor Smirnov-Golovanov and asked us to convey her greetings to him.

CARMEN CONNECTION

THERE WAS ONE more surprise in store. The next day after class, encouraged by Ludmila's statement that, of the 30 leading roles she had danced in her career, Carmen had been her favorite, I showed her a short Carmen-inspired solo one of my teachers had choreographed for me for a recent competition. As I had hoped, Ludmila gave me some very good

Feeding a Whisky Jack in our "backyard."

corrections—and she and Victor must have liked what they saw because the next morning, Mr. Robertson had still more news for me: MCB wanted me to dance the role of Carmen in the ballet *Carmen Suite*, which they would return to their repertoire if I came to Moscow. By the end of the week the dream had grown: MCB was eager to establish a connection with the Vancouver ballet community, and they wanted a pair of Canadian dancers. Rebecca Blaney was invited to join the company along with me.

A meeting among my parents, Victor, Ludmila and Mr. Robertson was scheduled for the following Sunday. By the time we all gathered on Irina's patio to discuss details, I hadn't slept in two days. It felt like a dream world, but practical matters brought it down to earth. It was decided that Dad and I would go to Moscow as soon as our visas came through. I would have only three months to train with the company in Moscow before leaving in October for MCB's five-week Asian tour of Taiwan, Hong Kong, Singapore and Manila. The sooner we got there, the better. In those three months I was expected to learn all of *Carmen*, and, along with Rebecca, Tall Swan in *Swan Lake*, various parts for *The Nutcracker*, including a solo each for Rebecca and me, and, if time allowed, *Cinderella* Stepsisters and Lilac Fairy. After the Asian tour we would return to Moscow for five weeks' training before departing on a tour of Wales and northern England. A holiday would follow, then performances in Moscow and preparations for another possible tour.

MCB would help us find an apartment in Moscow and complete the technical training I was leaving several years early in Vancouver. Over the expected two-year commitment I would be paid a stipend in rubles for the training weeks in Moscow; while on tour I would be paid a principal, soloist or corps dancer's wage, depending on the role performed, in U.S. dollars or Pounds sterling. I would receive an allowance for food and would stay in decent hotels. My only question was, "When do I leave?"

Within days of that Sunday meeting Victor and Mila (as I now called Ludmila) had flown back to Russia, leaving two families in a state of great excitement. Rebecca's family had been doing its homework too — something her grandma, Jean Orr, was particularly well equipped to do. A former ballerina, she had been Canada's first "Giselle," and she still played a big part in the Vancouver dance scene. Rebecca was 17 and had received

most of her training from a local school, but for the past year she had been a student at Seattle's Pacific Northwest Ballet School. Originally from West Vancouver, she was already accustomed to living away and following a correspondence-school program.

At home, the log cabin in the forests of Hollyburn Mountain.

HARDY BEGINNINGS

MY FIRST HOME was a log cabin in the forests of Hollyburn Mountain, rising above West Vancouver. I was born on February 7, 1984; my brother Dylan was three years older. My first few years were divided between the cabin and Granville Island, part of Vancouver's waterfront, where my parents owned a kayak shop and ran a magazine. My cradle was a kayak hanging from the shop's ceiling, and my first toddling ground was the nearby farmers' market with its wide variety of kneecaps and sticky patches of squashed fruit. When I was old enough, Dylan and I ran around the docks looking for starfish and rats among the boats moored at the marina.

When I was four, my family moved from the cabin (*La Maison Verte*) to a rented house in the city (*La Maison Grise*). The combination of my parents' growing businesses and Dylan's school schedule didn't fit well with mountain living, which required chopping wood for the stove and hiking home through snow with the groceries for almost half the year. *La Maison Grise*, where we stayed for about two years, had its attractions, such as the treasures a geologist neighbor regularly buried in the alley behind his house for kids to find. Our backyard had a trampoline, an apple tree that produced two kinds of apples, and a fine tree house from which the occasional water balloon was launched. We were known in the neighborhood as the people with the big dogs: Neblina and her son Benji, our two Great Pyrenees, had moved down from the mountain with us.

Before I started dancing, at age six, my parents had sold the businesses on Granville Island, and we moved back up to the mountain. From now on the cabin would have a flush toilet—no more creepy monsters in the outhouse at night—and electricity from a generator. Dylan and I were given a choice: we could get a TV, or, if we preferred, we could keep the trampoline. We picked the trampoline.

OPPOSITE PAGE
My Dad, me and Dylan, off to school. (Beatrice Dowd)

ABOVE
Me and my brother Dylan.

FIRST DANCING SHOES

WHEN I SAW my first performance of *The Nutcracker* at age six, I decided, like every other little girl in the audience, that the only thing in life was to become the one in the pink tutu.

My first few ballet classes were at a community center with a grumpy lady and a pianist who made you cringe. After a little research, Mom came up with an address for the Goh Ballet Academy, which taught mostly the Vaganova technique. The school was in a nice old building with pink awnings, big studios with floor-to-ceiling mirrors and pink velvet curtains. What made it even better was that it was full of older students we could watch dance after our own class. On top of that there would be lots of productions and performances, even for the little kids.

For the next eight years, the school became my second home. In 1991 I did my first performance—as a snowflake in the Christmas show—and one year later, at eight, I made the cut to be a bug in Pacific Northwest Ballet's touring production of *A Midsummer Night's Dream*. This was serious business as we got to perform on the stage of the Queen Elizabeth Theatre, the largest performance space in Vancouver at the time. In 1992 I was one of a dozen pink-tutued ballerinas hired to assassinate President Yeltsin in a spy movie called *Black Cat 2.* Our scene was shot on the stage of Vancouver's other big theater, the grand old Orpheum—and I got a $54 paycheck.

The following October, Dylan, who was starting Grade 8, and I, a fifth-grader, became homeschoolers. Until then we had both been in the French Immersion program. Now we made a dramatic switch to English, reading every English book we could lay hands on. Mom had to bribe us with the full set of Gaston Lagaffe comic books just so we'd keep up our French. (I'm glad of this because French proved surprisingly useful to me abroad, later on.)

The "real" books we had to work with included school texts, lots of novels, a self-explanatory math book especially conceived for homeschoolers, and the journals we both kept. We shared a computer with Dad, who by now had become an author of children's books and worked at home so he could supervise and cook for us. Mom worked downtown for a newspaper.

By what was now the fourth year in my ballet training, I had been taught by many teachers, both during the year and in the summer program. All had been good and very kind, except for one who was good but not kind. I remember one particular occasion when I stood in the studio with my left hand on the barre and right foot *coupé en arrière*, all eagerness to please. Mrs. X, always a stickler for technique, took one look at my effort and walked away snarling that I was hopeless. *Hopeless:* I cried myself to sleep that night, but after that my skin began to thicken—enough so that by the time I earned my first and somewhat dismal mark at a ballet competition I was able to shrug and say: *Pfff. The adjudicator made a mistake.* In time I realized that whether she had intended it or not, Mrs. X had helped me deal with that kind of hurt, and I thank her now. Besides, she was right about the *coupé en arrière:* I still get corrected on it!

That year and the next I tried my foot at soccer with the formidable

Playing a candy cane in an early performance.

Me as a bug in A Midsummer Night's Dream.

West Van Ladybugs. From my position in defense, waiting for the play to heat up so I could kick something, I often had time to think about ballet. Cleats, I discovered, give somewhat the same support as pointe shoes, so I could practice walking about in the mud on the tips of my toes.

This helped my mental preparation for the next big show, which came not long before my eleventh birthday: I auditioned for Ballet West's Vancouver production of *The Nutcracker,* and got in as an Oriental Servant. This is when I first came to know Rebecca Blaney—and those were the first of many *Nutcrackers* we were to dance together.

It was on the last night of these performances at the Queen Elizabeth Theatre that I had my first traumatic stage experience. The group dance was about half done when I felt an odd, loose sensation about my waist. I was wearing a pretty red costume with a silky blouse and short velvet pants, topped with a big puffy turban. The loosening I'd felt was not my imagination: my pants were coming undone—a shocking turn of luck because I was wearing a bright green bodysuit underneath (in defiance of a costume lady). One sharp fellow performer was kind enough to remark in a loud whisper, "Olympia, your pants are falling off!", which promptly made everyone on stage look (or so it felt). Running around struggling with arm movements, holding my pants up with my knees, I saw the Sugar Plum Fairy burst out laughing when she spotted my little green backside. I got through the dance somehow, only to find myself face to face with the costume lady backstage.

Fortunately that first mishap was soon followed by other firsts that did more for my dignity: my first win at a ballet competition, my first performance on pointe (in the corps of *Swan Lake,* Act II, in the school's end-of-year show), and my first solo on pointe, as the Baby Doll in the school's production of *The Fairy Doll.*

AT 12, CURIOUS about high school, I went into Grade 7, which in West Vancouver marked the start of secondary school. I did the whole year in a special half-day program designed for kids involved in sports or the arts. This worked out well so I went on to Grade 8, but by mid-October it occurred to me I no longer had time to read (my second passion after ballet), that I'd lost ground with my math, and that I'd been happier at home with Dyl. So I went back to homeschooling.

Family friends who spent time with us made major contributions to our education, especially the three Johns. Among them they had enough knowledge and skills to start a school from scratch, and they had a habit of turning up with the books we were just ready for. There was also Sid, the mountain elder who moved in with us for a time and helped us build a couple of extra rooms for the cabin, including the loft that became my bedroom. (From my window I could see as far south as the U.S. San Juan Islands, 50 miles away; and at night the lights of Vancouver twinkled for me.)

OPPOSITE PAGE
Ready for my corps role in La Bayadère.

ABOVE
With my Dad in Lighthouse Park.

ABOVE, INSET
My brother Dylan.

Dance followed me everywhere, even on hikes into the interior of British Columbia.

FROM SYLPH TO FEMME FATALE

MEANWHILE AT BALLET, there was always something to prepare for: if not studio or public performances, then exams, competitions, or fundraisers. For the first three years I was pegged as a slight, sylph-like creature darting through misty woods in fluffy costumes. I was in danger of becoming typecast, but in 1997 it was as a sylph that I won the junior British Columbia championships.

Less than two weeks into our usual summer break, I began rehearsals for a newly choreographed group dance. The school would be presenting it, along with a number of solos, at a big international conference at the recently opened Chan Centre for the Performing Arts. A day before the

show, I was asked to fill in for an injured soloist and so performed as a sylph again, relearning a dance I would be doing on pointe for the first time. The evening of the gala arrived and I was the most frightened I'd ever been on stage. Luckily, trembling hands were part of the choreography. I learned from this that I could trust my body to remember the steps even when my brain flashed terror messages.

Just before my 14th birthday, my teachers let me tackle the female solo from the Grand Pas Classique, after much begging on my part. I'd learned part of it from a guest teacher the previous summer and wanted the challenge. I almost passed out after the first rehearsal and killed a pair of pointe shoes in less than an hour, but eventually I got the steps nailed down. More importantly, that spring I went from sylph to *femme fatale*

One of my early solo performances as a sylph.

with my solo *Carmen* number performed in a red-and-black corset and a short black wig. This was enormous fun to learn, and I was congratulated on my sex appeal by the competition's adjudicator!

Soon after this, there were preparations for the school's 20th anniversary gala, our June 1998 end-of-year show. A lot of the pieces we senior students worked on for the event were also to be used on a five-city tour of China planned for August. I was really excited about the tour; it was the first I'd be old enough to join. Rehearsals for new pieces were going to start during summer school in July, in a couple of weeks' time. By the end of the first week of vacation, I was quite ready to start dancing again. That's when Mom spotted a little notice about a Vaganova seminar at the Russian Community Centre, and my life took another path altogether.

Rebecca and I were a good match, both tall for dancers at 5'7".

RIGHT
Interview with CBC Radio-Canada before leaving for Russia.

FIVE WEEKS, A LIFETIME

I ATTENDED SUMMER school while waiting for Dad's and my visas to arrive. This took not the expected ten days but a full five weeks — ample time for proper goodbyes to the old ballet school and to the family cabin, which was to be put on the market in the fall.

While Rebecca and I waited we did interviews for television, radio and the papers. The most intimidating was a morning interview with Radio-Canada—the French-language arm of the Canadian Broadcasting Corporation—for which I had to relearn my French overnight. I was also starting to learn Russian from Irina Carlsen-Reid. She gave me some of her Russian ballet videos to watch (including Alberto Alonso's *Carmen Suite,* danced by Bolshoi star Maya Plisetskaya, for whom the role was created in 1967). She also advised me on what to pack and supplied me with some of her suggestions, including several pairs of gift pointe shoes.

A few days before I left for Russia, my teachers and friends at the school held a goodbye party in one of the studios. I was given a delicate porcelain music box adorned with angels that turned to the music of Pachelbel's *Canon.* I packed it along with family photos, a small album of pressed flowers from the mountain, a horseshoe I'd carried back from a ten-day hike near the Yukon border, Dominique, my stuffed mouse, and enough wine gums to last me a year. There was also a book called *Come Hell or High Water* by transatlantic sailor Claire Francis, a former dancer.

Finally, departure day came and, heart thumping, suitcases bulging, I took my leave. From the airplane, Dad and I watched Vancouver become smaller and disappear as we circled the city on our way east.

Part 2

Apprenticeship in Moscow

OPPOSITE PAGE
"Waltz of the Flowers" in
The Nutcracker.

AT SHEREMETEVO airport, Dad and I wheeled our suitcases out of Customs and into a wall of hot, stuffy air in the arrivals hall. Victor and Vlad, the company's assistant manager, were there to meet us. Vlad spoke English well, which spared me from having to greet them in my rehearsed Russian.

An oppressive smell of stale smoke, vodka, cheap cologne and Russian food permeated the terminal building. Outside it was hotter and even more clammy. Our hosts had hired a driver in a small, nondescript car to take us into town. In the parking lot the car was blocked by two rows of similarly-occupied vehicles, so we had to wake up grumpy drivers and squeeze by our neighbors before we could drive away into the twilight.

Only a never-ending stream of billboards advertising McDonald's, Coke and Marlboro in bold Cyrillic print interrupted the drab landscape

on the way to the city. Clusters of buildings resembling discarded boxes merged into a suburb of apartment blocks that paralleled a broad road. It was so wide it might have accommodated six lanes each way, if they had been indicated. There seemed to be no road rules in place other than speed and natural instincts. The cars were mostly clunkers like ours but there were also luxury sedans with dark glass and cell phone aerials: "Mafia or diplomats," Vlad explained.

Buildings got older and grander as we neared the center. Peter's Palace, a red-and-white fairytale vision with its huge onion dome, flashed by on the left and a huge outdoor stadium loomed just behind it.

Then we were downtown, traveling along a well-lit and prosperous-looking avenue filled with people scurrying about with their shopping. All was quiet and dark, however, as we approached our new home among the narrower streets of the city's old quarter. We pulled up to a big, ugly cement-and-glass building surrounded by a fenced-in playground. Inside, the lobby was fiercely guarded by two *babushkas*—not a species of grandmother one messes with. We entered a weary elevator that creaked to the sixth floor, where we found ourselves in a dimly lit and very grim hallway. Loose floor tiles tinkled as we walked. The doors on either side were big and solid, with padding and serious double locks. My neighbor's doorway was scarred by burn marks and shattered cement, indicating where it had recently been blown open.

Our tower was built by the government during the 1960s, to house dancers and musicians of the Bolshoi. Though the building had been privatized a few years before, many artists had remained in the apartments, buying them up at modest prices. Victor and Mila lived upstairs.

We were soon joined in the corridor by a grubby-looking man who introduced himself as my landlord, Pavel. He spoke French and lived immediately above us with his elderly mother.

Pavel let us into our apartment: a main room with two sofa beds, chairs, a table, a small TV and a large wall unit. There were strange, dark paintings of ballet sets on the walls, placed there by Victor. The small kitchen had hospital-green tiling, a thick old sink, a tiny table with three chairs, a gas stove and a good-sized refrigerator. The toilet was separate from the bathroom, which contained a sink, a washing machine that doubled as a dryer, and a full bath.

OPPOSITE PAGE
St. Basil's cathedral, Moscow.

BELOW
Me and Rebecca, strolling the streets of Moscow.

The kitchen and main room shared a balcony and both had huge, triple-glazed windows covered by lacy curtains. From here we had a view of the Canadian Embassy's yellow walls across the street and beyond it, in the middle distance, the illuminated spire of a skyscraper.

Pavel showed us how everything worked, but when the kitchen tap was turned on it gasped, rumbled, choked and, as we all backed away, spewed forth a most foul-looking rusty liquid. It had clearly been a while since anyone had leased this apartment. Mila had come down to welcome us, but as it was quite late, Dad paid Pavel the first month's rent in American $100 bills (no receipts) and we said goodnight to everyone. I went to sleep feeling more than a bit disoriented.

Women selling hand-knit mohair shawls in the market at Arbat.

OPPOSITE PAGE
Shopping in Old Arbat.

Rebecca and her father had arrived earlier and were settled in an apartment much like ours, three floors down. The next morning, Vlad took us all on a neighborhood tour, pointing out some of the tiny, often unmarked food shops and bakeries along the crooked streets. The street names would take some getting used to: the sign for our street, Afanasievsky Boulevard, read like upside down spy code. A restaurant, pronounced *res-tah-rahn*, was written *pectopah*; a cashier, pronounced *kahs-sah*, was a *kacca*. It was a good thing Irina had given me *Learn Russian in 10 Minutes a Day*.

The Old Arbat, a pedestrian shopping street five minutes from the apartment, was lined with ornate buildings and alive with buskers, por-

trait artists and souvenir vendors. Running roughly parallel to it was the New Arbat, a wide avenue with a supermarket and department stores. I was pleasantly surprised by how well stocked the supermarket was. It carried my favorite shampoo, Dad's McVitie gingersnaps, Haagen Daaz ice cream—and everything at much the same prices as at home. Fruit, vegetables and meat were expensive, but the local flour and bread very cheap. There were no long line-ups or empty shelves, but people thought nothing of bumping or pushing to get to what they wanted.

In many of the streets around us renovations were underway on the old buildings still to be found amidst the modern apartment blocks. Under the faded blue or yellow plasterwork some were made of squared logs. Many had intricately carved wooden doors.

Everything we needed was within easy reach, including two bustling metro stations. There was visible police presence on the neighborhood's avenues, but the men in uniform seemed to worry more about checking papers than stopping drivers reversing at full speed down the one-way side streets. There were many little parks around us, with seemingly more dogs than children visiting them.

Police presence on the streets in Moscow.

JET-LAGGED REHEARSAL

Down time, carefully stitching my pointe shoes.

STILL FEELING jet-lagged, we returned to our apartments so Rebecca and I could get ready for class at two that afternoon. I was nervous and knew I wouldn't be able to dance my best with a body that was half-asleep. I could see the studio from my window: it occupied the top floor of a school building. Rebecca and I walked over with Vlad, passing through a back-street maze of crumbling brick walls and archways to the schoolyard and across it to the building's rear entrance, a dark stairwell that smelled of tomcat. Higher up, windows revealed walls at different stages of peeling and decay, displaying their past colors in a curly edged camouflage pattern.

We arrived at the top of eight flights of spiraling stairs quite breathless, ducked through a tiny door, and found ourselves in a gymnasium: a huge studio with a vaulted ceiling, slanted mirrors, a barre and a grand piano. We were met by a tallish man with wild, fluffy hair who was introduced as Vitus, the stage hand. Vlad left and we followed Vitus through another door and up a very dark, steep staircase past curtained rooms. He showed us into a small loft overlooking what proved to be the dressing room for the corps de ballet. Rebecca and I felt a bit out of place when we realized we were sharing the principals' dressing room.

As dancers came in to the studio, they glanced curiously toward us as we stretched in the corner. Most of the girls warming up alongside us wore colorful bodysuits with stripes or polka dots, and, instead of the soft shoes I was used to, soft blocks with white bobby socks. They all looked like serious workers but several seemed overly thin. All twenty male corps dancers disappeared downstairs for their own class, while the half-dozen male principals and senior soloists joined ours. Soon Mila and Victor arrived, escorted by Piff, their cocker spaniel.

Class was challenging because of my jet lag, nerves, the heat and my attempts to watch the rest of the company as I danced. Mila didn't make things easier by putting Rebecca and me front and center with the senior soloists and principals. And of course she saw *everything*, even when her head was turned the other way. The pressure was on: the other dancers, apart from already knowing most of the repertoire, had a month's head start on classes and rehearsals for the season. We were new, and the youngest in the company.

I was introduced to Mila's use of negative reinforcement and some favorite English phrases: "It's no good," "It's very bad," and "What is it?

OPPOSITE PAGE
An early class at the Moscow City Ballet studio.

OPPOSITE PAGE, INSET
Ludmila helps me with a pose.

ABOVE
The first-day jitters wear off.

35

You like it? No!" The raised eyebrows and droop at the corner of her mouth helped send the message, which she delivered frequently, and no less forcefully, to others in Russian. This wasn't the warm, enthusiastic Mila I had worked with in Vancouver. Other dancers addressed her in the formal Russian manner, known as patronymic. She was Ludmila Fyedorovna (meaning Fyodor's daughter); Victor was Victor Victorovich.

I felt a bit better when we got to pirouettes and jumps. I actually heard a quiet "It's okay," granted with a dismissive shrug. Some of the dancers spoke English quite well, but they didn't let on immediately. They were friendly, though there were sidelong glances and occasional giggles. Most MCB dancers, we'd been told, were Moscow-trained, but many had come from Perm, Saratov, Novosibirsk or one or another of the former Russian republics. Mila herself was from Odessa, Vancouver's sister city in the Ukraine.

After class Rebecca and I watched a rehearsal for Act II of *Swan Lake*. The corps was impressive and the principal, Natalia, technically outstanding. Mila moved the rehearsal along, wasting no time. Before we knew it we were being introduced to our fellow Tall Swans—Victoria, Elena and Irina—and getting started on the Tall Swans dance. The choreography was straightforward and the rehearsal went well.

Finally, Mila, Victor, Vitali Lurie (the company manager) and Larissa (our accompanist) cleared the studio so that I could begin to learn the second solo for *Carmen* in relative privacy. The process turned out to be harder than I expected, for as well as learning new and unusual steps, I was required to *act* the part immediately. Russians, I came to understand, see themselves as actors first, dancers second; the body is there only to tell the story. I hadn't approached a part quite this way before, and I was daunted. On top of this, Mila was pushing hard to make up for lost time. I was so tired by the time I got home I fell asleep sitting up with my feet soaking in the tub.

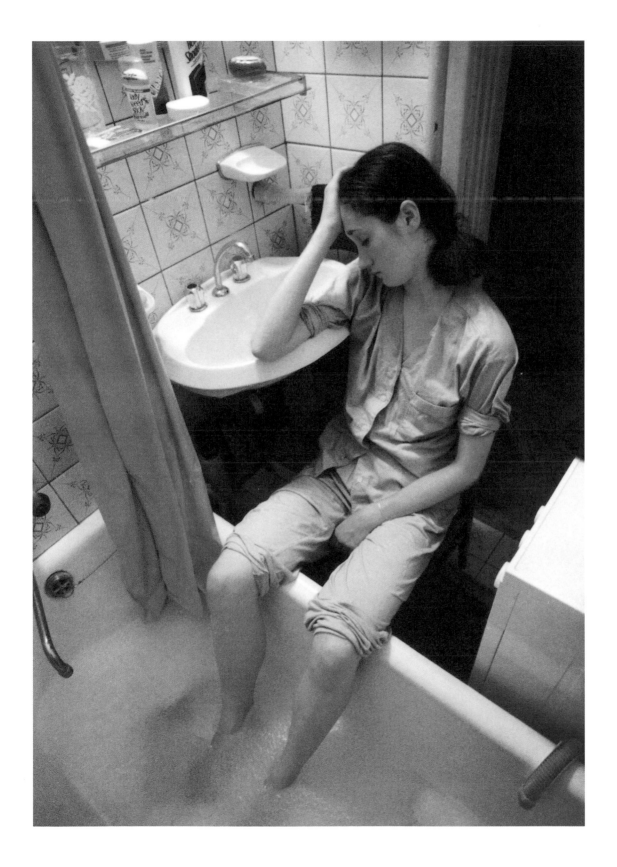

OPPOSITE PAGE, ABOVE

Starting Carmen rehearsals.

OPPOSITE PAGE, BELOW

*I'm getting to know
Carmen better.*

SOLOS AND DARK EYES

IT DIDN'T TAKE long to fit into the company's schedule. Each day we started with class at two, followed by hour-long rehearsals until eight o'clock. Rehearsals took place six days a week, with Mondays off. The company had a masseur who came twice a week. Sessions with him were a treat, but walking down the worn stairs after he had done your legs could result in a tumble if you weren't careful.

Early on, when Rebecca and I had not yet learned their names, we made up nicknames for our dancing companions: Smiley, Bonerack, Coffee, Blondie, Legs, Skeletor and Hercules—enough to baffle anyone overhearing our animated but cryptic discussions. We indulged in the usual ballet game of figuring out who was gay and who was straight—a wasted effort in this company, since straight was all they hired. Everybody seemed either married, *with* someone, looking for someone, or juggling all three. So much so that a warning had come down from Victor Victorovich that any male caught flirting with the Canadians would be fired.

I don't like class very much, I remember grumbling in a letter to my friends in Vancouver: *too many double à la seconde turns, backward grands fouettés, adages en demi-pointe and other tricky moves done in front of class.* There was also the galling fact that all the other dancers seemed to have 180-degree legs. Still, class was becoming more manageable and I was learning a lot very fast.

Early in the month, rehearsals had started for the Waltz and Coda in *Swan Lake*, corps for *Cinderella* and *Sleeping Beauty*, and my various roles (parent, rat and Waltz soloist) in *The Nutcracker*, but mostly I was busy with *Carmen*.

The ballet Alonso had choreographed in Moscow more than thirty years before called for a cast of four female and three male dancers, plus a male corps of eight or more. There were four performances of *Carmen Suite* scheduled for the Asia tour, so the pressure was real. Not only was the ballet in need of revival after six years, but we were going about this without understudies for the main roles or any sort of second cast. It was a huge risk to take on an unknown 14-year-old.

In the two months before the Asia tour I had to learn two long solos, two *adagios* (romantic pas de deux) with Don José, one with the Toreador, and three long scenes with the whole cast. I would be on stage for most of the 50-minute ballet. Aside from Carmen, the female roles were the dual character of Fate/The Bull and a matched pair of cigarette girls, one of whom was Rebecca.

While I was learning the steps, *Carmen* rehearsals were the last session of the day after most of the other dancers had gone home. It was a relief to not have an audience, and Mila was nicer when it was just us.

I had trouble sleeping the night before my first rehearsal for the *adagio* with the Toreador when it was announced my partner would be Gulam, a man with intense dark eyes that scared me silly. He was born and trained in Azerbaijan, was 35 and married to a retired dancer. His 18-year-old stepdaughter Kira was a corps dancer with the company. Before the first rehearsal he said jokingly that he hoped he wouldn't get put in jail for doing this dance with a 14-year-old. The pas de deux we shared was not the sort of dance you did with a man 20 years your senior with his daughter watching. It didn't help my concentration that everyone watching burst out laughing the first time we did it, or that every time one of us started giggling it grew into such a laughing fit that we had to stop the music until we could breathe again.

41

*An intense moment with
the Toreador.*

BLACK LACE AND MATRIOSHKA DOLLS

NOT LONG AFTER we arrived in Moscow the weather turned cold, and on August 11th Dad came back from the shops with a thick new duvet for my bed. It was so cold in the studio that I brought my hot water bottle with me to class every day to thaw my gel toepads. Later on the weather became so unpredictable that I went from woolly sweater to tank top to woolly sweater again. I also got to try on the *Carmen* costume Mila had handed down to me, all black lace and silk fringes. It had been worn also by Bolshoi star Nadezhda Pavlova, whom Mila had coached in the role.

Dad, meanwhile, kept busy buying things for the apartment, cooking for three (after her father left, Rebecca shared meals with us), and making daily trips to MCB's office in the school's basement to e-mail Vancouver. He also worked on the revisions to his newest children's book and photographed our rehearsals. During days off we did manage to see the sights, including the Kremlin and the Pushkin art museum, both of which were within walking distance of the apartment. Gorky Park was a bit unkempt, its fairground tacky and vaguely menacing, but the day we spent there was beautiful.

I made shopping forays in the neighborhood and started a *matrioshka* doll collection. I investigated the street-corner kiosks that sold everything from candy to vodka, lurked around the theater supply store down the block, had my portrait done by a sidewalk artist and visited the ladies selling hand-knit mohair shawls on the Arbat. I shopped for my new food favorites: a German yogurt so delicious I had trouble giving it up even after I found out it had ten percent fat content, and tiny buns filled with cabbage and egg, rice or fruit preserves. They were called *piroshki,* and we bought them warm from one of the hidden shops near our house for a ruble each (U.S. 20 cents).

Adding to my collection of matrioshka *dolls.*

During our more leisurely mornings at home I read, fixed pointe shoes, and kept up my journal. I was too busy to feel homesick, but I badly

43

*Fitting the black-lace
Carmen costume worn by
my predecessors.*

45

missed having a cat. And I was anxious about the dancing, biting my fingernails down to the quick every second day.

There was much to be done in preparation for the tour. Vlad and other company staff rushed around the office getting visas, arranging for costumes and sets to be shipped, brochures prepared, tickets bought. The e-mail flurry was fierce.

THE ROLE OF *Carmen*'s Don José had initially gone to the company's lead male, Dimitri, but he stepped on a nail so wasn't able to dance until it had healed properly. In addition, his nose was reportedly out of joint as a result of being passed over for the Toreador role, a great favorite among Russian leading men. So Don José went instead to our other Dimitri, a good-natured soloist affectionately known as Dima Two. As with Gulam, Dima and I had a difficult time trying to rein in our laughter during the cozier moments.

Mila was demanding but a true expert at teaching repertoire quickly, demonstrating everything with precision and flair. She knew every step and nuance and had the most expressive arms I had ever seen. One on one she was candid, eager to pass on her knowledge and capable of warm encouragement as well as harsh criticism. When her smile came through it was like sunshine.

Because Rebecca was unwell, our joint Stepsisters rehearsals had been postponed, and instead I began working on steps for the fairy corps in *Cinderella*. The relative ease and camaraderie of corps rehearsals made them especially enjoyable; in fact, compared to *Carmen*, everything seemed like a breeze. I had fun with company members. They laughed at my attempts at Russian, and as their English was no better, the least little bit of conversation turned into humorous exchanges.

In the world around us, President Yeltsin had fired his cabinet, and the ruble had gone into freefall. Russians lined up at the banks attempting to access their frozen funds. Dad began to stock up on food staples amidst foreign press forecasts of runaway inflation and import shortages. We held U.S. dollars, so things were cheaper but less available. Still, I had no difficulty finding dancing and costume supplies. I bought two pairs of pointe shoes from the Bolshoi: a house make at $3 and Grishkos at $10.

In the arms of Don José.

Rehearsal with Dima Two
as Don José.

COUNTDOWN

WITH THE START of September, the school housing our studio reopened for daytime classes and our dance training shifted to evening hours, with a 6 p.m. start. Often there were rehearsals upstairs for *The Nutcracker* or some other ballet with Victor, while I had rehearsal with Mila downstairs in the other studio, reached by way of a big central staircase leading off to a long hallway with tall paned windows. The only light came from outside. Feeling my way down the worn stone steps in the dark,

Getting closer to Carmen.

then walking from one square of moonlight to another, I could hear the music coming from the studio and the *clop clop* of my pointe shoes on the old wooden floor echoing off the high ceiling. The only fear I had then was for what was to come in the studio: *Carmen* rehearsals were progressing, but slowly, and although I knew the steps and was able to act, it was never enough for Mila. "It's okay, but it's Olympia, not Carmen," she would say with her trademark shrug. With just over a month to go before the Taiwan premiere, Victor said I was doing fine. If I was looking for positive reinforcement from Mila it wouldn't come, he added. She was on Carmen's side more than mine, and she was looking for perfection.

Mila had also told me I would have to lose weight. I had never had reason to worry about my weight or what I ate, so this threw me into a panic. I rushed out to buy a scale: the needle settled at 53 kilograms (117 pounds). "You're not the least bit overweight for your height and the last thing we need here is an eating disorder," Dad said in fury. We knew a dancer with severe anorexia and had seen how heartbreaking the effects could be. An emergency meeting with Mila revealed that my male partners were having trouble lifting me, a problem linked more to my height than my weight, although my weight did challenge the decades-old Bolshoi rule: 52 kilograms was the limit at which a ballerina's partner had the right to refuse to lift her, for their mutual safety. Losing a kilo—two at the outside—didn't seem too unreasonable to me, so I gave up the ten-percent-fat yogurt and

49

piroshki and cut down at meals as much as Dad would let me. Dieting and the new anxiety around food conflicted with my body's needs: I felt hungry all the time. This led to bingeing and dieting, which altered my metabolism and energy flow, frustrated me, and took ages to get under control.

Meanwhile, the ruble was down again after a short recovery. The papers said consumer prices in Russia had increased 43 percent in the first two weeks of September alone. Many basic goods stayed the same price, however, and so became ridiculously cheap for foreigners. On the street, Russians were bearing up as well as could be expected; this wasn't the first crisis they'd been through. However, there was talk of starvation for the outer regions of Russia in the coming winter, and there were increasing fears of civil unrest. We began to see more soldiers around. The Canadian Embassy had worked out an emergency evacuation plan, just in case.

ON THE FIRST Sunday of autumn we performed *The Nutcracker* just outside Moscow. The setting for my initiation with the company was nothing grander than a slightly run-down theater in a grim, concrete town, but it felt great to be on stage. Our production was easy to enjoy, and the families in the audience were very receptive. There were enough pink tutus flying around that stage to make a lasting impression on any six-year-old.

After curtain call, Svetlana, the principal, and Rebecca, Dad and I (as foreign visitors) were invited to a reception with company staff and the director of the theater. It was a lengthy affair involving ponderous speeches and endless toasts with glass after glass of *shampanskoye* and vodka. At one point the director was almost moved to tears by the toast he was giving to Victor—something about the importance of the arts.

Some days after our first *Nutcracker* (we performed two more a week later), I was told I'd be doing the ballet's Arabian solo on the U.K. tour in December and January. For Asia, there was no longer the time to learn Lilac Fairy or *Cinderella* Stepsisters, but Rebecca and I were shown a video and told to make a start on Stepsisters. I'd become sufficiently comfortable with *Carmen* that I felt this was manageable. We were ready for full *Carmen* run-throughs. The first half of the show would consist of principals Natalia and Stanislav doing the *Romeo and Juliet* pas de deux, and

ABOVE
*My debut performance with
the Moscow City Ballet in*
The Nutcracker.

RIGHT
Another scene from
The Nutcracker.

principals Svetlana and Anatoly in *Russian Souvenir*, a folklore-flavored piece full of acrobatics.

In the first days of October, after Moscow had had its first powdering of snow, we had a last *Carmen* rehearsal. There was press in attendance: Paula Newton, CTV's Moscow correspondent, had brought a camera crew for a *W5* segment. Rebecca and I each sat for an interview, to be supplemented later with post-Asia tour coverage.

When we were together, Rebecca did most of the talking, Russian or English. She was a classic extrovert charging into life; I tended to be guarded, more reserved, wearing blinkers to stay on track. Hardly peas in a pod, but we had lots of laughs together and were often mistaken for sisters.

Dad, meanwhile, had found a new line of work: he had landed an assignment with the Canadian Embassy, which was then undergoing renovations, and until we left for Asia he spent a good part of his day watching Russian workers to make sure they were not planting bugs in the plasterwork.

In preparing to leave I attended to some last-minute errands, rushing to the theatrical supply store to get just the right length of fake eyelashes and a few pairs of gypsy-colored tights. I was silly with excitement and nervousness. This would be my debut on the road and I was both terrified and eager for it to begin.

OPPOSITE PAGE, ABOVE
Interview with CTV'*s Moscow correspondent after our final* Carmen *rehearsal.*

OPPOSITE PAGE, BELOW
Me and Rebecca on the road with the Moscow City Ballet.

Part 3

Asia Tour: Under the Lights

TAIWAN

ON OCTOBER 6TH the artistic staff and cast for *Romeo and Juliet*, *Russian Souvenir* and *Carmen Suite* left for Taiwan. Dad was booked on a separate flight, and the rest of the company would follow two days later. Our flight to Hong Kong felt painfully long because, on Aeroflot, smoking was not prohibited. Emerging like smoked hams into the giant new Hong Kong airport, we boarded a huge, nearly empty China Airlines plane for the connection to Taipei. There a bus picked us up for the drive south to Taichung, a large city halfway down the island, for the start of our tour. We were travelling in air-conditioned style, with extra pillows and a TV showing second-rate American movies.

Outside my window a foreign world whipped past: a kaleidoscope of steep jungle hills with farms in the valleys, women working in the fields

OPPOSITE PAGE
Performing Carmen *in Asia.*

55

wearing wide cone hats, muscled truck drivers leaning out of the cabs of heavily loaded trucks, and Chinese-language road signs intermingled with tall, thin billboards. Towns grew beside the road like clusters of mushrooms – grungy and tired-looking conglomerations with streams of scooters and cars pouring into main streets. Dirty factories interspersed with the occasional posh home behind high walls dotted the outskirts. There were rivers too: wide, wild stretches of gravel with tiny streams meandering beneath storm walls built against sudden floods. Taiwan's population is over 20 million and today they all seemed to be on the road. In fact we saw whole families balanced on scooters. At roadside stops the air outside was so hot and humid our skin felt like it was dissolving.

Our schedule (neatly typed on World Touring Productions letterhead) read: first 16 days in Taichung, Kaohsiung, Tainan — two hotels, six theaters, 12 performances (three *Carmen Suites*, four *Cinderellas*, five *Swan Lakes*.); last four days in Taipei — one hotel, one theater, six performances (three *Swan Lakes*, two *Cinderellas*, one *Carmen Suite*). Taiwan total: 18 performances in 20 days.

We weren't going to be bored!

Exploring the streets of Taichung.

TAICHUNG'S NARROW sidewalks were congested with produce and vendors. The air was loaded with strange smells: exotic cooking, overripe fruit, cologne and sour drains. Rebecca and I unloaded our gear into a surprisingly pleasant hotel room. Even after a long day, the two of us were more excited than tired, so we headed to the 7-Eleven across the street for a celebratory Slurpee. (Amazingly, there are 7-Elevens everywhere in Taiwan, with one main difference: the overwhelming whiff of poached preserved eggs as you open the door.) On either side of the convenience store were restaurants with trays of exotic-looking food in their windows and little dark shops that mended clothing or made electronics.

The next day we had the first of many press conferences. We smiled for reporters while a translator talked about us, and I had to traipse around in the atrium of a huge mall wearing my *Carmen* costume while a mob of photographers snapped pictures. A second press conference took place backstage at one of Taichung's large theaters. As "Carmen," I was being

In costume at a press conference in Taiwan.

introduced alongside the company principals, which felt distinctly odd. It helped that I was in full costume and able to hide behind my make-up.

On October 9th we packed up and headed to Kaohsiung, a big city on the island's southern tip, and checked into an even more luxurious hotel. The souvenir program to accompany our tour was equally glamorous. The two Canadian names looked incongruous among the rest, and I was even more startled to find in it a glossy double-page photo spread of me dressed as *Carmen*. Our first performance would be the following night in yet another town.

59

OUT OF THE WINGS: CARMEN DEBUT

AT NOON ON the 10th, we headed for Chayi, a long bus ride that swelled my feet and numbed my legs. I had my headphones and a much-used *Carmen* tape with me, so the time wasn't wasted. On arrival at the theater, the cast got ready quickly for a warm-up class. The stage, to my relief, was big and smooth. Barre exercises felt like I had someone else's legs on backwards, but by the time we got to center exercises my legs at least felt like my own. Because it was the premiere, Mila had us rehearse the whole show, which helped ease my jitters.

Our make-up artist, helped by Mila (who stood giving instructions from behind), reshaped my nose with various shades of blush and made my lips so big I couldn't look in the mirror without a giggle. Every time someone new came into my dressing room they'd suggest a bit more lip would be good, and by the time we were done I looked like some kind of exotic fish.

The show started. *Romeo and Juliet* and *Russian Souvenir* went by so

quickly that before I knew it the curtain had closed for intermission and *Carmen* was next. I had begun warming up behind the wings, trying to fast-forward through the whole show in the few remaining minutes. This left me quite winded and feeling tipsy from hyperventilating. Then five minutes to curtain was announced backstage.

The music for *Carmen* has a 70-second prologue before the curtain opens. On this occasion, however, perhaps because the stage crew was as nervous as I was, the curtain went up with the start of the music, leaving me standing poised and purposeful in my opening pose, one foot on pointe in the spotlight, with the men in corps arranged in a semicircle around me—cracking jokes in the shadows. This gave me a good long time to consider the audience. My left foot was almost asleep by the time the prologue was

OPPOSITE PAGE
A quiet moment before our last
rehearsal and my debut as
Carmen.

ABOVE
Ludmila helps me get ready.

61

Waiting for the premiere.

over, but fortunately it behaved itself when the time came. The rest of the performance felt like a very intense, colorful blur. Everything went approximately as planned except that in the *adagio* with Gulam, the looped fringes of my costume got hooked on the buttons of his matador suit and I couldn't release from an embrace without the front of my costume pulling away, leaving the two of us staring down my body suit for a tense moment until a loop or button gave.

I messed up curtain call by running on stage too early and realized suddenly that I had no idea how I was supposed to bow, but I managed to get the flowers okay. Then, hearing from someone that I was to bring Victor Victorovich out on stage to bow with us, I went off to find him behind the wings, only to realize, once my eyes had adjusted to the dark, that only Vlad was there: Victor was out front videotaping, and I should have been taking my last bows in front of the curtain.

It was a relief to have the premiere behind me, and at long last Mila was happy. I was looking forward to the next day's performance because there were details she and I both wanted to fix, but for now my mind was at peace.

32 FOUETTÉS AND A TYPHOON

THE SECOND *Carmen* performance was at the Kaohsiung Cultural Centre and the third in the Taichung Centre; both were good theaters with excellent stages. By the third performance, the other half of the company had arrived and came to watch. Fortunately all went without a hitch (except for the loop *vs.* button thing, which Gulam was now solving by snapping the loops off). Backstage after the bows Mila declared this had been my best performance. She had even cried at the end, she said, an admission that might have made me cry also had she not remembered a correction at just that moment.

As well as performing, some of the dancers participated in master classes Mila taught at local dance schools to promote our tour. These classes were often difficult because we were still adjusting to the heat and humidity. At one of the larger ballet schools the class had more than a hundred students, and at the end Mila asked Natalia, Svetlana and me to demonstrate 32 *fouettés*. Masses of extra students were crowding around now, but I almost didn't have time to be afraid. The pianist gave us our cue and the three of us were off, swirling round and round to the music. We all finished in sync—to enthusiastic applause. Then word spread about my

age: I was mobbed by a small sea of students giggling about my height and white skin, touching me to see if I was real. I hid my overwhelming urge to run behind what I hoped was a demure smile.

Our performances of *Cinderella* and *Swan Lake* went well, but they were accompanied by a change in the weather: a typhoon was sweeping Taiwan. Sheets of gray rain lashed the streets and buildings, and palm trees bent in the wind. In the morning, bits of trees and buildings lay scattered across the road: going out to my favorite bakery became quite an adventure. The weather didn't stop the theater-goers, fortunately, and at the peak of the storm there was a full house in the theater and we danced while roof panels banged in the wind.

Flights were being canceled. After one failed attempt, Dad caught a plane back to Canada on the 16th. I'd be on my own until Taipei, but I was

64

OPPOSITE PAGE
Preparing for Swan Lake.

ABOVE
The corps de ballet in Swan
Lake.

in good spirits. Gulam had been asked to keep an eye on me, as he did on his stepdaughter Kira, and my room-sharing arrangement with Rebecca was working quite well.

To fill the hour or two it takes to come down from the energy high left after curtain close, I sometimes dropped in on the parties held most evenings in various dancers' rooms. The Russians would dig into their suitcases for the canned fish, fake cheese, chunks of lard, huge sausages, heavy dark bread and tea they'd brought from home. They lived off those supplies for the whole tour, saving all the money from their food allowance—except for what they needed to buy vodka along the way. These gatherings were noisy but fairly tame compared to the average high school party: for one thing, I saw no drug use. I did learn key Russian swearwords, though, and gradually I was able to make out more and more of the conversations and jokes.

Some much needed rest in my hotel in Taichung.

I had one major post-performance crisis to handle after returning to our hotel room late one night. Dominique, the much-repaired stuffed mouse I had inherited from Dylan in childhood, was nowhere to be found. I panicked, searched my mind for where I had last seen him, and decided he must have got mixed up with the sheets when the beds were made. I immediately ran to the front desk. Batting false eyelashes, lips still smeared with stage lipstick, I proceeded to explain to the little man in the suit that I had lost my long-legged mouse in yellow suspenders. A search was called and within hours, Dominique was back in bed, unharmed after a ride in a laundry truck.

DR. SUN YAT SEN MEMORIAL HALL

Our venue in Taipei, Dr. Sun Yat Sen Memorial Hall.

WE MOVED NORTH to Taipei and settled into yet another swish hotel in one of the capital's lively commercial neighborhoods, and happily there would be no bussing for a while. We were within walking distance of our venue for the next six shows, the Dr. Sun Yat Sen Memorial Hall–a particularly grand theater surrounded by manicured gardens.

Rebecca's parents were in Taipei for a two-week stay with the tour and Mom arrived not long after. Although she could stay only a few days, she would see me do my last *Carmen* performance in Asia. I moved into her room and we caught up on three months of chatter. Mostly we did quiet things—reading and fixing up pointe shoes—and when they were finished we poked around the neighborhood, meandering through the maze of little streets behind the skyscraper-lined avenues. The streets were teeming with scooters, but the local culture seemed hidden behind a façade of American chains: 7-Elevens, Starbucks, Starbucks-wannabes, designer clothing stores. American music blared from the storefronts, yet surprisingly few people spoke any English. At the hotel, the man at the desk called Mom "Sir."

BELOW
Ludmila and her Carmen enjoy
a triumphant moment.

OPPOSITE PAGE
In character.

A second typhoon hit the island. There was a deluge of warm rain and the hotel's glass entrance was barricaded against the wind.

Between the *Cinderellas* and *Swan Lakes,* we fit in much-needed *Carmen* rehearsals. We would be dealing with an intimidating audience when we performed at the 2,300-seat Dr. Sun Yat Sen Memorial Hall: the seating was so steep that from the stage it looked like a solid wall of people. Plugged into my Walkman, I spent as much time as I could collecting my thoughts before the big night.

To my relief, the performance went fine, and when it came to the applause, it didn't hurt that half the dancers in the company were in the audience. "You have conquered Taipei," declared our impresario as he pumped my hand. Victor beamed and Mila was "*very* happy." This was *her* Carmen, she said, and for the first time she marveled that she'd managed to teach it to me in so little time. Afterwards, in the dressing room, she gave me the silver and amethyst ring she was wearing.

THE CARMEN STORY

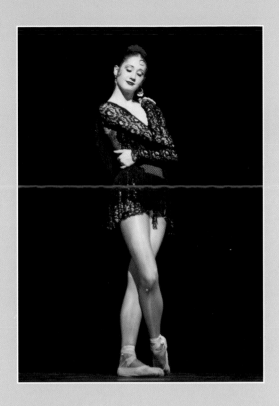

Carmen had her origins as the title character in a short novel by French author Prosper Mérimée. Published in 1845 and set in southern Spain, *Carmen* was the story of a hot-blooded, free-spirited gypsy woman whose fateful entanglement with a jealous soldier named Don José brings her death by his hand. Like those of Spain's Don Juan and Don Quixote, the powerful character and story of Carmen have endured, inspiring countless retellings. Besides Bizet's famous opera *Carmen*, created in 1875, there have been Carmen plays and Carmen movies by the dozens, including one by Cecil B. De Mille in 1915 and another by Charlie Chaplin the following year. Rita Hayworth starred in *The Loves of Carmen* in 1948.

Barely a year after Mérimée had created Carmen a century and a half ago, she had inspired a first ballet: *Carmen et son Torero* by Marius Petipa, who was then a young choreographer in Madrid. Dozens of other choreographic treatments have followed, in flamenco, neo-classical and modern dance. Among the more enduring works is Roland Petit's *Carmen*, a full-length ballet created for Les Ballets de Paris and first performed in 1949 in London. Renée (Zizi) Jeanmaire's urchin hairstyle in the title role started a new fashion and remains integral to the character in the Petit version.

KARMEN SUITA

The Carmen in Moscow City Ballet's repertoire is the one-act, 50-minute *Carmen Suite* choreographed by the Cuban Alberto Alonso for Bolshoi star Maya Plisetskaya in 1967. *Carmen Suite*, or *Karmen Suita*, is set to music re-scored from Bizet's original by Plisetskaya's husband, Russian composer Rodion Shchedrin. Plisetskaya's dramatic portrayal of Carmen, reportedly her favorite role, helped confirm her as a legend and the ballet soon took its place as a landmark in the Bolshoi repertoire. *Carmen Suite* was adopted later by many other Russian companies. In Cuba, a slightly different version of *Carmen Suite* became a signature piece for Alicia Alonso, and is still today part of the repertoire of The National Ballet of Cuba.

DRAMA IN THE BULLRING

The ballet's action takes place in a bullring around which are seated masked individuals representing a faceless crowd of spectators. Carmen makes her entrance; the spectators invite her to join them but she defiantly refuses: she is not one of them. She is a participant, a risk-taker, a free spirit: she wants to live as she wants, without a mask.

A soldier, Don José, and the Corregidor, his superior, enter. There is a changing of the guard in which the soldiers' faces are impassive, their movements stiff and mechanical.

Don José is left alone to his guard duties. Carmen approaches him. She mocks his wooden stance and, by teasing and taunting, attempts to release him from the blank conformity he represents. She succeeds and he tentatively joins her in a dance.

The *tabatchkis*, two of Carmen's co-workers from the tobacco factory, come on stage, followed by soldiers. Fate, in the guise of a bull, causes a violent fight between the three women. Carmen is blamed and José leads her off to prison, but in the end agrees to let her escape.

Next comes José's solo, a dance full of torment and yearning for her.

Some time elapses.

OPPOSITE PAGE
She seduces him
through dance.

Carmen watches as the Toreador
enters the ring.

RIGHT
Me and Gulam in the intense
adagio.

OPPOSITE PAGE
With measured concentration,
Gulam lifts me.

The *tabatchkis* appear moving in perfect unison, dancing to syncopated hand-clapping by the soldiers/spectators.

The Toreador enters the bullring; Carmen watches him, impressed by his splendor and courage. He is like her, living a life of risk.

Powerfully drawn to each other, they dance a measured, stylized adagio in which their wills clash in a combat of equals.

The Corregidor enters and watches their dance angrily; he too yearns for Carmen.

Don José reappears, stripped of uniform, disheveled, looking for Carmen who has all but forgotten him. A stand-off ensues between José, the Toreador and the Corregidor. Carmen has to choose between them. She turns to the Toreador but he walks away with angry pride.

Later, alone with José, she reassesses her feelings. She has created his need for her and understands their fates are intertwined. (In Mérimée's book and Bizet's opera, Don José, his military career ruined for enabling her escape, has joined the band of smugglers Carmen secretly works with.) They dance a pas de deux in which her mood evolves from cool indecision to passionate abandon.

OPPOSITE PAGE, ABOVE
Me and Gulam, eyes locked as Fate lurks in the background.

OPPOSITE PAGE, BELOW
Carmen has to decide which of the three men she will choose.

LEFT
Carmen and Don José, their fates intertwined.

Carmen and Don José in an
impassioned embrace.

OPPOSITE PAGE
Carmen is tormented by Fate.

In the Card Scene, Carmen draws her death card. Although a free spirit, she is not free of superstition: she foresees her own death by Don José's hand, and as Fate dances around her she is filled with fear. She runs into the arena, where the Toreador begins fighting Fate/the bull. José appears, furious and desperate as the Toreador, reunited with Carmen, takes up her defense. There is a struggle. José grabs Carmen. She resists. Fate, then Carmen rush toward the Toreador.

At the very moment the Toreador succeeds in overcoming the bull (Carmen's fate), José intercepts his lost love and stabs her. Carmen stands before José. Death has won. Carmen touches José's face tenderly to show she forgives and understands. She walks a few steps, attempting to resume her proud opening pose, but collapses in José's arms.

OPPOSITE PAGE
Stabbed by her former lover Don José, Carmen collapses in his arms.

ABOVE
Death has won.

EAST AND BACK

AFTER *Carmen,* Mom went back to her job in Vancouver and I flew to Hong Kong with the company for the next leg of the tour. Though we stayed right downtown, we had all too little time to see the city. We did three performances in four days, leaving one afternoon off, which we spent as a group at an amusement park across the bay. A ride on the park's chairlift revealed a skyline we couldn't have imagined from the canyons of gray concrete around our hotel.

While at this hotel I was twice accosted by older men, a Westerner in each case, who struck up amiable conversation about the company, Russia and the like, then proceeded to hand me a visiting card (photo and name only) while inviting me down later. *Hmmm.* Was our hotel listed in some sort of sex guide to Asia? Or worse, did dancers have a reputation for "entertaining"? I hurried off quickly the first time, and the second time Gulam, my fierce guardian, turned up at just the right moment to give the man the eye.

One of the better things about Hong Kong was that with all three performances being of *Cinderella,* the stage was set for making a start on Stepsister work with Rebecca after rehearsal, when there was time. Already this was enormous fun.

In early November we moved to the quiet, clean and very green world of Singapore, with a day off spent at the Botanical Gardens, smelling the flowers and posing for photographs with the handsome but bilious black swans ruling the pond. The streets around our hotel and the Kallang Theatre, our venue, seemed eerily empty after the crowds of Taiwan and Hong Kong. One afternoon I did happen upon a busy place, a market and outdoor eatery where I was offered (and declined) a live frog to barbecue for a snack.

OPPOSITE PAGE
In the dressing room in Taipei.
(Beatrice Dowd)

83

WEARY FOR "HOME"

ON THE SCHEDULE for our short stay in Singapore were two performances of *Swan Lake* coupled with a celebration for MCB's 10th anniversary. Champagne flowed and various dignitaries attended, but by then I was too tired to appreciate the "glamour" of touring life. The supplies of pickled fish and Russian tea were running out and a general weariness was setting in.

Our final stop was an eight-day stay in Manila, in a hotel so pleasantly posh it made me miss the city altogether. Buried in a cocoon of luxury— huge beds, marble bathrooms and overly solicitous service—I felt little inclination to break out for anything but our rehearsals and performances at the Meralco Theatre. When I did venture out it was merely to the mega-mall attached to the hotel. There I was stared at constantly–so tall and so white!

Our last two performances of *Swan Lake* were preceded by two *Sleeping Beauties*, my first opportunity to see MCB's *Sleeping Beauty* in full. From my easy spot in corps, I could keep my eye on the Lilac Fairy role that I hadn't had time to learn in Moscow.

By then we were all so worn out that we just wanted those shows done with, but the audiences were unfailingly polite in their appreciation. Throughout the tour, audiences were never rowdy: success was gauged by the length of applause rather than its intensity. But applause was not enough: I longed for the simple comforts of my little apartment in Moscow. I was sick of travel, sick of the heat and bustle of Asia, and all my pointe shoes were worn through.

On November 14th, 60 of us left for Moscow via Bangkok. In five weeks we had done 27 performances in ten different theaters. We'd earned our rest.

*Signing autographs for
a friendly crowd.*

FIRE AND ICE IN MOSCOW

A BLAST OF cold air and swirling snow met us as we came off the plane in Moscow. We dashed from the plane to a semi-derelict bus and I stowed my suitcase and hurried inside. (Planes don't taxi up to the terminal in Moscow; passengers are driven from the plane to Customs in either a wheeled refrigerator or a mobile sauna, depending on the season.) Once through Customs, we slipped and slid across the parking lot to another freezing bus. I was chilled to the bone in my cotton pants, runners and track jacket, so I rolled myself into a ball against some hand baggage and buried my head in my mohair shawl from the Arbat.

After what seemed like hours, we set off. After a while I noticed that pleasantly warm air was pumping through the aisle. In fact—*sniff, sniff*—the rear half of the bus was filling with smoke! We pulled over. There were ominous creaks and groans and then, all of a sudden, flames licked up the outside of the window I'd been resting my head against. We rushed out and watched from a safe distance, our feet in the snow, while the driver extinguished the flames. Eventually we all got on again, expecting the worst, but the rest of the half-hour trip into Moscow was uneventful. Walking the two blocks from the bus to our building, half-carrying, half-dragging my bags, felt like it would finish me off, but as I turned the key and walked to the alcove where my lumpy bed and feather duvet waited, an enormous relief swept over me.

The next few days I spent sleeping and getting the house ready for Dylan, who would be joining me for the five-week training period before our U.K. tour. It was minus 17 degrees outside and the cold was accompanied by blasting wind that stung my face with snow, so the errands that needed to be done were done quickly. As much as I looked forward to seeing Dyl and showing him around Moscow, after the long

Ready for the cold weather in Moscow.

weeks of group travel and room-sharing I found being on my own quite blissful and wasn't overly concerned when problems cropped up with his visa application. I buried myself in books and caught up with my journal. There were daily phone calls from Canada to check up on me and keep me posted regarding Dyl's likely arrival date.

The morning after our first rehearsals Rebecca called to tell me to look out the apartment window to our studios. I put my head out and my chin dropped: the whole top floor was in flames! The fire department was soon on the scene, and they were able to confine the fire to the top floor (our dressing rooms and studio), but it burned all day and long into the night. The heating had apparently been turned up too high to make up for the severe cold, and something had gone wrong with the wiring. The day before, most of us had returned our dancing gear to the dressing rooms. Now nothing was left: personal effects, the grand piano, the sound equipment, the mirrors and floor were down to cinders. Fortunately, costumes and most of the sets, including *The Nutcracker* set we would need for the U.K. tour, were safe in the company office in the basement. The Canadian Embassy had had serious worries about the fire spreading to their side of the street, and because of the smoke they'd had to cancel the Canadian Foodfest/*Souper Canadien* slated for that evening.

I needed replacement warm-up gear, soft shoes and pointe shoes, and I was escorted to one of the city's ballet supply stores hidden underground in the back corner of the last in a labyrinth of residential courtyards.

STUDIO MOVES

REHEARSALS FOR THE U.K. tour were moved first to an old, overheated dance hall with a bumpy, slippery floor. The next day we upgraded to an underheated studio where the floor was virtually corrugated but had a proper non-slip surface. Changing studios meant having to get further acquainted with Moscow's huge metro network, which had its good and bad points. The ticket gates threatened to crack your kneecaps together with two fast-moving metal bars if you moved through at the wrong speed, and if you passed this test and were not trampled on by the thronging masses or lost in the labyrinth, you had to beware of the train doors squeezing shut with people caught in the middle. But apart from these exciting quirks, the trains were reliable, quick and cheap. In addition, many of the stations looked like palace halls, with heroic murals and statues from the Stalin era.

By now we were well into week two, and Dylan still hadn't arrived. Back home everyone was getting a bit frantic about the visa delay. I paid a visit to the people I knew at the Canadian Embassy. Knowing I was on my own, they had been very supportive of me since my return to Moscow, checking up on me regularly. They promised to look into the problem and help out if they could. Paula Newton and her CTV crew provided an amusing diversion, with more interviewing and filming for the *W5* story.

I began rehearsals for Stepsister in *Cinderella*, Acts I and II of *Giselle*, and the Spanish solo in *The Nutcracker*. I had had to switch from the Arabian to the Spanish solo because two dancers had left the company after the Asia tour and I became a replacement. There was less than a month to prepare, so the schedule was arduous. I also had to learn a demi-soloist part for the Dream Scene in *Don Quixote*. This was for a single show on the outskirts of the city, and I hoped Dylan would arrive in time to see it.

Mila insisted that Rebecca and I enhance our acting in the mime sections of Stepsisters by talking and screaming our parts, a new and creative way to embarrass us and subject us to mental anguish, it seemed at the time, but the portrayals were sharper as a result. Rehearsals for the dance sequences were more relaxed and invariably hilarious. As for *Giselle*, Act II was problematic because Rebecca and I, as the Wili soloists Morna and Zolma, had to dance in front of corps using the same steps, but we could never quite get the timing to coincide with their movements. When the lines of corps crossed each other hopping on one leg, we were always either a foot behind or a head ahead, because of our height. Mila finally conceded that we should place ourselves so most of our bodies lined up — and hope for the best.

FLAMENCO IN THE KITCHEN

I HAD BEEN ALONE for almost three weeks when news came that Dylan was on his way, and by then the excitement of living by myself had

well and truly worn off. I eagerly hired a car and driver for the trip to and from the airport, and the company's manager escorted me in case we had any problems. Dylan, wearing his goofiest smile, emerged from Customs tottering under a huge backpack and a heavy-duty case containing Betty, his cherished flamenco guitar.

The two of us made good use of what time we had: starting with our out-of-town *Don Quixote* performance, I took him everywhere. A few days into his stay we were invited to dinner by Elisabeth, the French lady next door, and toasted the event with Dylan's first shot of vodka, which made him blotchy. I took him to all my favorite spots, and even found out the girls behind supermarket counters were capable of smiling.

Dylan was terribly serious about his music and practiced at every opportunity. When "Betty" developed a hairline crack in the dry, over-heated air of the apartment, he took to playing in the bathroom, door closed, with the hot tap running. This brought relief: *Carmen* or not, I still had my doubts about flamenco in the kitchen.

For a cultural treat Elisabeth took Dylan out to the Tchaikovsky Concert Hall to hear Rostropovich, the famous cellist, in a birthday concert for novelist Alexander Solzhenitsyn. Solzhenitsyn was there, sitting not three feet away from Dylan.

Dyl had brought me some novels he'd enjoyed but also a sports nutrition book with strict instructions from Mom to make me read it. I did and had soon created not only a better diet, but also a thousand excuses to stray from it. I cooked all the delicious foods I craved and watched Dylan eat them until he began to rebel about being overfed, a concept I couldn't grasp at the time.

In mid-December, news came from home that our cabin had been sold. My parents were on their way to London to meet up with us for Christmas. They planned to buy a van like the one we'd called home on a previous trip to Europe when we were little.

I was nervous about my tricky Spanish solo, but time was up. On the winter solstice Dyl and I were off to Wales and England.

OPPOSITE PAGE
My brother Dylan in Manege Square in Moscow.

89

Part 4

U.K. Tour: Second Debut

WALES

THE U.K. TOUR would keep us busy from December 20th to January 30th, with 43 performances over 30 working days (plus five days for travel and five days off for Christmas and New Year's). The first three weeks were in Cardiff, Wales; the balance was in the northern England cities of York, Sheffield and Manchester. We had four ballets on the program: *Cinderella* and *Sleeping Beauty* (as in Asia), plus *Nutcracker* and *Giselle*. Whereas in Asia we'd had live accompaniment only in Hong Kong, here we'd be working with the National Ballet Orchestra throughout. A company called Victor Hochhauser was hosting the tour.

After the Moscow-London flight, we travelled west by bus to our new base in Cardiff, a newish hotel close to St. David's Hall, our venue. Every street in the old town was festooned with Christmas lights, the shop

OPPOSITE PAGE
Me and Rebecca rehearsing the Stepsisters dance from Cinderella.

*Christmas shopping with Dylan
in Cardiff.*

windows flashed color and glitter, fat turkeys with frilly garters lay heaped in the indoor market, and everyone looked happy in spite of weather that seemed to range from drizzle to light snow. Dylan had flown out of Moscow a day before and met up with our parents in London. The three had driven to Wales to meet me in a bright red vw campervan. I lived at the hotel, room-sharing with Rebecca once again, but I met my family for meals and sightseeing. Dylan was more than happy to switch to the warm acoustics of our tiled bathroom when Rebecca and I were at the theater. She too was having visitors: her mother and grandmother had joined her for the holidays.

St. David's was large and new, with a good dressing room and stage. Like the rest of Cardiff, it was proudly Welsh, with all announcements made in Gaelic as well as English. The six *Nutcrackers* we performed there before the Christmas break had packed houses and the audiences were warm and lively.

I spent Christmas with my family, not in Wales but in central London, at the home of our friend Christine. We exchanged presents beside a tiny live tree festooned with favorite ornaments from home, feasted on roast partridge, and took a leisurely stroll through Hyde Park, which was nearby. Boxing Day, however, we were back in Cardiff, where the company was preparing for a run of 16 shows—mainly *Giselles* and *Cinderellas*.

At St. David's Hall in Cardiff.

93

PRESS CLIPPINGS

D'ARCY CLAYBOURNE REVIEWS THE MOSCOW CITY BALLET

Moscow City Ballet are certainly making their presence felt in Wales. If their new productions of *Giselle* (December 29–30) and *Cinderella* (January 2–7) are half as entertaining as their splendid performance of *The Nutcracker*, they will certainly be long remembered by their Cardiff audiences.

Making the most of the intimate St David's Hall arena, the company gives *The Nutcracker* that magical touch right from the start with a stunning yet simple Christmas Tree backdrop. Clever lighting is used to create the effect of snow and to conjure a mischievous mood which the children in the audience clearly found appealing. The Mouse King, the Sugar Plum Fairy and the Nutcracker Prince are all brought to life with skill and grace by one of the world's leading ballet companies, who certainly enjoy their craft.

They also enjoy the applause, and the immense pride and passion of this 80-strong company shines through at all times. The famous, memorable music is magnificent. The National Ballet Orchestra, conducted by Igor Shavruk, are absolutely first class and will no doubt excel themselves in the coming weeks as well. *Giselle* promises to be quite a treat, offering the full force of the Russian dance tradition. . . .

Moscow City Ballet was founded in 1988 by the distinguished Russian choreographer Victor Smirnov-Golovanov. The company's greatest success has been in the UK, where it has given more than 800 performances since 1991, accompanied by the National Ballet Orchestra.

(27 December 1998, *Wales on Sundays*, Cardiff, U.K.)

AUDIENCE HAS A BALL AT THE FAIRYTALE BALLET

Moscow City Ballet's Christmas visits to Cardiff have become as traditional as turkey and mince pies. Judging by the full house at St David's Hall for the first night of *Cinderella*, ballet goers still have a strong appetite for the classical favorites. This year's production had all the ingredients to keep the audience happy, including glittering costumes and set, which transformed the sterile surroundings of St David's. Natalie Shelokova was everything a Cinderella should be. Her dancing had an ethereal delicacy, a wonderful contrast to the power of her prince Mikhail Ronikov. Every pas de deux was delightful.

It was a bright, colorful production. We were spared the dark drudgery of Cinderella's down at heel existence in her step-family's house. Instead, the ballet concentrated on the flamboyance of court life and the antics of the ugly sisters. We were taken on a journey through the Middle East and the Island of the Corsairs before a joyful finale when the prince rediscovered his bride. It was the stuff fairytales are made of.

(22 December 1998, *South Wales Echo*, by Margaret O'Reltly, Cardiff, U.K.)

ABOVE

Stepsisters rehearsal with Rebecca.

GIANT SLIPPER AND SOUR NOTES

AFTER *Carmen*, *Cinderella* Stepsister became my favorite role. Rebecca and I could let loose with hair-pulling, kicks and other antics on stage, and then head back to our hotel room laughing. Once we had the timing and sequences clear, we could improvise, so no two shows were the same.

Letting loose as the mischievous and playful stepsister in Cinderella.

ABOVE AND OPPOSITE PAGE
More scenes from Cinderella.

PAGES 98-99
The stepsisters' final bow.

Sometimes, when we felt inspired, we rehearsed new moves in the hotel corridor at night. In one scene we had to force Cinderella's little slipper on over our own pointe shoe and jump around uncomfortably to acknowledge the bad fit. Our shoes were too big for the tiny slipper to stay on long enough, so I prepared a substitute, one of my very old, heavily epoxied pointe shoes now gussied up with paint and sequins. At the next performance, when the prince leaned over to pick up what was to be the matching pair of Cinderella shoes, he burst out laughing at the sight of my oversized glue-sodden slipper.

Having the live orchestra was occasionally a mixed blessing: as the holiday spirits flowed, so the merriment of some of the musicians grew. A French horn player and his friends used intermission as an opportunity to knock back a quick pint so that in Act II, a sour note or foghorn blast would startle the dancers and set the audience squirming.

For New Year's break, between *Giselle* and *Cinderella*, the family drove north to the Brecon Beacons hills, where we stayed in a country inn surrounded by sheep paddocks, stone walls and sleeping gardens. After a long hike to a neighboring hilltop, from which we watched specks of light settle across a velvet-green valley in the gathering dusk, I fell asleep before midnight and had to be woken to drink my champagne. I nodded back to sleep immediately; no time for New Year's resolutions.

With Dylan on New Year's Eve
in the Welsh countryside.

NORTHERN ENGLAND

ON JANUARY 10TH the company moved to York. We had seven performances scheduled during our week at the Grand Opera House but only one matinee, leaving the mornings free for exploring. With little more than my corps role in *Sleeping Beauty* to preoccupy me (we did six *Sleeping Beauty* performances and one *Giselle*), I felt particularly able to enjoy the city's beauty and historic buildings, among them the cathedral of York Minster and Clifford's Tower, the 13th century ruin just across from our hotel. (Less successful was the visit Rebecca and I made to the York Dungeon and its ghoulish displays on torture and the plague.) My wanderings were curtailed only when the River Ouse rather dramatically overflowed its banks, rising all the way to the theater's stage door. My family was gone by then: Dad and Dylan had left for southern Spain to look for

guitar teachers and Mom had returned to Vancouver until the four of us would reunite in Seville at the end of the tour. Everyone in the MCB was getting February off.

Sheffield was next, and our new base was The Swallow, a mansion set in its own garden with a pond, a swimming pool and a sauna—an oasis in what seemed like a slightly dismal industrial city. To add to the luxurious feeling Rebecca and I even took to ordering breakfast in our room. Nutrition book cast aside, I had taken to eating only one meal per day, breakfast (yogurt, fruit, toast, juice and tea) and then bingeing later in the day. My body craved chocolate. It was probably just nerves: we had seven performances of *The Nutcracker* on a stage that had a slant of more than seven percent and was very narrow, which made everything horrible. It also caused the outside of my ankle to hurt from the added rolling of my foot in the Spanish solo.

OPPOSITE
My Zolma solo in Giselle.

ABOVE
A corps scene in Act Two of Giselle.

FINAL STRETCH

January 24th ushered us into downtown Manchester with another seven performances to do in six days: two *Sleeping Beauties* and the final five *Nutcrackers*. The Palace Theatre had a mercifully huge, flat stage, as if to make up for Sheffield's nightmare. I was pacing myself for the last stretch.

I had found the U.K. tour more pleasurable than the Asia tour: aside from the easier travel, the surroundings were less perplexing, the food and climate comfortingly familiar, and the language stress-free. Here I could understand, be understood, and interpret for others for a change! It gave me a sense of freedom and control I hadn't felt in Asia. Still, the feeling in Manchester was much like the feeling in Manila: deep weariness, with every one of us counting the days left. Here as in Manila I saw the hotel, the theater, and no more than a block around them. I did manage a little jogging now and again (anything for a change), but I felt emotionally drained and there was little energy to spare. Luckily I hadn't had to miss any of the tour's forty-some performances, but by the last day my whole body was sore, once again all my pointe shoes were ruined, and even my suitcase was giving out. If I heard the music from *The Nutcracker* one more time, I'd scream.

After the last performance we boarded a bus for the four-hour drive to Gatwick airport—a miserable trip for me because the others blasted a Russian comedy video at us. Arriving at Gatwick at 5 a.m., Rebecca and I, bleary-eyed, said our goodbyes to the company, then went out for breakfast to celebrate the end of the tour. At seven we boarded the shuttle from Gatwick to Heathrow, where we parted company. She was off on the next flight to Vancouver, and I was off to Spain with Mom, who was waiting for me at the terminal. There were oranges on the trees in Seville, Dad had told her, and we were both ready to join the gypsies.

OPPOSITE PAGE
As a girlfriend in Giselle.

Part 5

Holiday in Carmen Country

THE PLANE CIRCLED over the soggy English farmland, then headed south for Spain. Soon we were looking down at a whole different world: a wide brown landscape of arid plains, plateaus and mountains with snowy tops in crisp, brilliant sunshine. Things turned greener as we got farther south and we spotted our first olive and orange groves.

Dad and Dyl were there to meet us at Seville airport, looking tanned and happy in their shorts and sandals. Oranges on the trees and the giant palms basking in the sunshine outside the terminal told my brain it was warm, but my body felt shivering cold. I was one tired girl. As a special treat, we spent the first night not in the hippie-gypsy van but in an old Seville hotel with a tiled inner courtyard and, more importantly, a proper bed with heaps of blankets to bury myself under.

OPPOSITE PAGE
Visiting Carmen's old haunts.

In the morning we all set out on foot to see the city. We found Carmen's old haunts: the huge old cigarette factory where she'd had her day job (it is now the university), and the Alcazar (the old city's fortified wall) where soldiers still hung out. We had morning coffee and our first taste of the local breakfast, a little crunchy bun filled with *jamon*, alongside the thick wall, which is now part of a park. Walking along it later we passed two soldiers on patrol: perfect Don Josés to have my picture taken with! We walked on to the prison Carmen had done her best to avoid and the bullring where she'd fought, and lost, her last fight with Don José. Everything was still there, 150 years after the Carmen story was created by Prosper Mérimée.

BIRTHDAY ROSES IN PARIS

A WEEK LATER we arrived in Paris, on the eve of my 15th birthday. We moved in with our old friend Alain in Montmartre. I was treated to birthday roses and gifts such as a ceremonial shopping trip to get genuine French underwear and my first real perfume, and tickets for the new *Astérix and Obélix* movie. As a birthday treat to myself, I cruised the streets around rue Lepic, sampling the beautiful little sweets in *confiserie* windows.

Shopping in Spain.

The best present was the prospect of three weeks in Paris (while Dad and Dylan headed off to Africa for a month). Because this was to be more than just a holiday, however, we immediately looked for a ballet school where I could do class four or five times a week to prepare for MCB's spring season. I also needed studio space in which to rehearse *Carmen* quietly on my own. I had to perform the ballet in a few weeks' time in Moscow—for me, the most daunting audience of all.

We found exactly what I needed on rue de Clichy, a short walk away in Montmartre. Much funkier than your usual ballet school, the Centre

International Danse Jazz was full of purple-haired people with rings in their noses, but it also had two Vaganova-trained teachers. I worked primarily with Dimitra Karagiannopoulou, who had left her home in Greece at 14 to study at the Bolshoi school in Moscow. She knew my building on Afanasievsky Boulevard, having visited a friend there many times. She understood exactly what I needed: her teaching helped my confidence and made me want to work really hard again.

Before and after my classes on rue de Clichy, Mom and I explored the city, mostly on foot. We took the metro to places like the Père Lachaise cemetery, the flea market and the Arab market. On our very first metro ride, a gypsy busker with his violin came up to me playing music from *Carmen*—as if he knew.

We explored the Butte Montmartre and, farther afield, the opera neighborhood, where we caught a performance of *Sylvia* by the Ballet de L'Opéra at the Palais Garnier. The dancing was as good as we'd heard, and the opera house very beautiful, but we had such terrible seats at the back of one of the boxes that we stood through the whole performance. We had better luck at a show given by a gypsy circus family under a big tent in Montmartre, with live music and song as much a part of the show as the jugglers, contortionists and trapeze artists.

In spite of daily visits to the *confiserie* for a small treat, I had managed to get my eating patterns sorted out *and* my weight back down to what it had been in Vancouver. I hadn't forgotten the threatening look Mila had given me as a goodbye when she told me that I had to be as skinny as her little finger when I arrived back in Moscow! After such a relaxed month I was all nerves at the prospect of the stress and hard work that awaited me.

Part 6

Moscow
Encore

IT WAS A COLD late afternoon on February 25th when we arrived at Sheremetevo airport. Heavy gray slush clogged the edges of the runway, its color a surprisingly good match for the sky and the surrounding buildings. Mom said it looked just like Montréal in winter. We pushed our way through with all our bags and found a taxi driver with an official-looking tag. After much bargaining we got a ride for only twice the normal rate to get to town. It was nice to get back to my little apartment, and although it was freezing outside, the building was pleasantly warm: heating is free in Moscow. Mom and I used my last three days off to take in some of the sights, braving the cold and icy sidewalks. The economic crisis had worsened, but there were still no shortages at our neighborhood stores.

OPPOSITE PAGE
Spanish solo in The Nutcracker.

Away from the city center, however, shelves were empty. We were getting 25 rubles to the dollar by this time, so a loaf of the most delicious bread cost 20 cents, a metro ride even less.

ONE OF THE first things we heard from Vlad at MCB's office was that en route from England, the ship carrying costumes, backdrops, sets and all of the dancers' ballet things had been caught in a storm. There was a lot of water damage, and the crate with all my belongings was lost overboard. Gone were the warm-up clothes and leotards I had replaced after the fire, along with all my little sentimental trinkets. I was really sorry to lose them, but my losses were nothing compared to the blow to the company. The walls and staircase of the office and storage area were lined with rumpled, stained costumes and props awaiting restoration.

We had our first class on March 1, as scheduled. It felt very short and insufficient after the two-hour sessions in Paris, something Mom agreed to remedy by booking private classes with Madame Zolotova, whom I had met years ago in Vancouver as a guest teacher. But it was good to see everyone again, looking well rested. Some dancers, I couldn't help noticing, had put on more than a little weight over the holidays; perhaps I could have got away with eating a few more of those Paris sweets after all. One new male dancer had joined us, and a former principal had returned after maternity leave.

That first day back in the studio there was a *Carmen* rehearsal with my new partner: Dima one, the company's senior lead, was back in the role of José, and he was on his best professional behavior. Everything went smoothly except for some minor choreographic miscues that were soon fixed.

A week later, on International Women's Day (a public holiday in Russia), I had the first of several technique sessions with Madame Z, the tiny, bubbly lady who had coached me and other Vancouver students in *Coppelia* a lifetime ago. Madame Z was very sweet and helpful: she hummed the class music to save us the expense of an accompanist, and later arranged classes to dovetail with MCB's. She and the company both worked out of studios in the former Imperial Theatre School, a block away

OPPOSITE PAGE
Spanish solo in The Nutcracker.

113

Another performance of
The Nutcracker.

from the Bolshoi and three minutes' walk from Red Square and the Kremlin. This building was where Victor had done his early choreographic studies. From the worn granite steps to the huge studios upstairs, one could sense the layers of history hiding behind the slightly musty, dusty smell. The studios alongside ours were used by Moscow Classical Ballet, another of the city's touring companies. (I had seen them dance *Cinderella* in Vancouver a year earlier.)

For *Carmen Suite,* we were practicing with new music because the original tape had been lost in the fire; this took some getting used to. The *tabatchkis* were also new; Rebecca, although back in Moscow, was still recovering from an injury sustained in Manchester. A complete backup *Carmen* cast was now being trained, which made for more social, less stressful rehearsals. In spite of the laughs, however, the rehearsal schedule felt very rushed.

SATURDAY IN ZELONOGRAD

WE PERFORMED *Carmen Suite* at Zelonograd, a good theater in the once secret "scientific" city just north of Moscow. Though the performance wasn't without its problems—the usual costume hitch plus a sudden hole in my tights—the adagio with José went extremely smoothly. I was not overly pleased with my own dancing but the Saturday audience clapped forever while Gulam, Dimitri and I stood bowing before the curtain. Victor liked Dimitri and me together, and Mila was pleased with the audience response.

This first *Carmen* was sandwiched between two performances of *The Nutcracker* at the Dietsky (the Children's Musical Theatre in Moscow)—performances that turned out to be unusually challenging. In MCB's version of Spanish solo I have to start with four penchés in 16 counts. These are tough enough to do on a good floor, but on one that is raked or badly corrugated like the Dietsky's, they are nothing short of nerve-wracking. At one point in the last *Nutcracker* I was swaying back and forth on one leg, just on the edge of control, my foot trapped in a hollow. For a moment I feared falling flat on my face, but my balance held, just. The Dietsky could be forgiven for its ugly floor and slight state of disrepair because it occupied a beautifully designed building set in a park near Moscow University. We had full houses and the audiences were wonderful. A good ticket cost 60 rubles, about $3. Prices were the same at the big Moscow Circus just alongside: $3 for a huge show complete with dancing bears and full orchestra.

CARMEN FINALE

As Easter approached I spotted a big blue-and-red poster in Cyrillic: *Karmen Suita*, it said, and below, in big letters, Karmen: Olympia Dowd, Canada. The season's last performance of *Carmen* fell on Good Friday, April 2—six months after my Taiwan debut. April 2 would not be Good Friday in Russia, however, where Orthodox Easter is celebrated a week later.

The show was staged at the Olimpisky, the theater of Moscow's former Olympic village, a large venue set among what was now a mixed assortment of buildings ranging from a shopping mall to a museum, surrounded by parkland. At last a stage that was big, flat and smooth at the same time.

For me, this final *Carmen* performance was both the most polished and the most satisfying. Everyone was happy as the curtain closed, and there were lots of hugs and kisses as family and friends—Gulam's wife and Kira, Dima's little daughter, Mom, and other smiling faces I knew—rushed backstage. Friends from the Canadian Embassy had come as a group, and there were more than enough bouquets to share that night. This was exactly as I might have dreamt it, and once we'd left the dressing rooms I still felt every bit the Russian prima in my outrageous stage make-up, surrounded by flowers and babbling companions on the metro ride home.

OPPOSITE PAGE
My final performance as Carmen for the Moscow City Ballet.

Celebrating the success of
Carmen *with Ludmila*
and Victor.

Afterword

MORE THAN THREE YEARS have passed and my story has come full circle: I am temporarily back in Vancouver, staying in shape and training for the next stage: a competition and tour in Brazil.

I left MCB in late spring of 1999, some weeks after that last *Carmen* performance in Moscow. A handful of performances had followed *Carmen*, but our season was showing signs of ending early. Two short tours had fallen through and several dancers had left the company to work elsewhere. At the time, I was expecting to return to Moscow to start training for MCB's fall season in mid-August, but those plans unraveled. Because of the tensions NATO military action in Kosovo was causing between Russia and the West, Victor Victorovich was half-expecting MCB's autumn tour across the U.S. to be canceled. "There could be a war," he said darkly. Domestic politics looked no brighter, with President Yeltsin threatening to impose a state of emergency in Russia in response to terrorist bombings blamed on rebels from the breakaway republic of Chechnya. Mom's Russian visa was expiring, and she wasn't about to leave me behind.

Our family reunited in a beautiful old farmhouse in the forested hills of Northern Tuscany, which we had the job of care-taking for a friend for several months. There were fig trees, olive trees, grapevines, 50 acres of oak and chestnut forests, three streams and a waterfall plunging into a jade-green swimming hole. The peace was broken only by the calls of cuckoos—and the roar of military jets tearing across the sky on their way to Kosovo.

Here I had time to catch up on some things I had been neglecting, including my home studies. To stay in shape, I took a daily private class in the nearby city of La Spezia with Barbara Lorenzini, a recently retired professional dancer. She was wonderful to work with—plus she spoke French, which helped a great deal.

When summer school season came, Mom and I left for Madrid, where I resumed more sustained training at the studios of Victor Ullate. (Victor Ullate was long a dancer with Maurice Béjart's Ballet du xxe Siècle. In 1976 he founded Spain's first national ballet conservatory, and later he was artistic director of the classical/contemporary company Ballet de la Comunidad de Madrid.) By then it had become obvious I would not be returning to Russia, where things had gotten worse, not better. A prominent theater director had been shot by the Mafia, the economy was still in shambles, and there were mounting tensions over Chechnya. Within weeks these would degenerate into a terrorist campaign that included bombing Moscow buildings, countered with systematic searches and counterstrikes. Foreigners were fleeing from the city.

My family decided to relocate to Madrid, where Dylan would take in a year of flamenco studies. So I became a full-time ballet student again, attending both the Ullate school and the Asociacion de Profesionales de la Danza, which put on a daily drop-in class taught by international guest teachers. I did Pilates exercises on the side to help my flexibility and strength, and settled down once more to my homeschooling and writing the first draft of this book.

After Spain we all went back to North America, and I found myself among Russians once again. I got a scholarship at the Kirov Academy in Washington, D.C., where I stayed half a year, studying with Alla Sizova and Ludmila Morkovina. I also took Russian language classes and finally learned to properly decipher Cyrillic.

At the Kirov I was given the White Swan pas de deux to do in the Xmas show, as well as the Lilac Fairy variation (at last!).

Offstage, however, my hips and back had been killing me and my balance and flexibility were off: something was definitely wrong. The problem had first appeared as a small imbalance in my posture, detected while we were still living in Italy. In Madrid, the imbalance had become detectable as a slight wow in my spine. I was sent to a physiotherapist, who sent me to a *traumatologico*, who decided the problem was slight, and that since I was still growing, we should simply have this looked at every six months or so—and in the meantime, here was a little insert to slip into my shoe to put me straight!

In the end I had to take some months off dance, then go through corrective retraining, which helped me get back on my dancer's feet. A fresh start—almost!

People often ask me whether or not it is a good idea to go off and do things like what I did when you're that young. I think it really comes down to a judgment call based on individual circumstances. If you do take on such a challenge, try not to let the excitement of the potential adventure blind you to the risks involved, even if that means putting a wet towel on your spirits. If you are working toward having a good long career as a ballet dancer, and a semi-normal life, I would say (reaching into my vast reservoirs of wisdom and experience!) go the normal route: steady, sustained training is a much sounder plan for both emotional and physical strength. Of course there are always risks, but it might be wise to save the big ones until a certain stability has been achieved.

I said yes to an exciting adventure, and that's certainly what I got! Great highs, some lows, a huge learning experience, and thanks to the brain function that remembers the good and fades out the rest, many lovely memories. Plus I'm only 18, and I have a lifetime of dance to look forward to.

Glossary

adagio: a ballet term borrowed from music, where it means "at ease" or "slow." Adagio is also used to refer to a romantic or slow pas de deux, performed together by a female and male dancer.

babushka: Russian word for grandmother or old woman.

Coda: from the Latin *cauda*, tail. The finishing segment of a pas de deux; also refers to the finale of a classical ballet in which all the principal dancers appear separately or with their partners.

confiserie: French for candy store.

corps de ballet: the main body of dancers of a ballet company who dance together as a group.

coupé en arrière: a movement that calls for the foot to be sharply pulled off the floor and placed in back of the ankle.

CTV: the largest private television network in Canada.

demi-pointe: indicates that the dancer is to stand high on the balls of the feet and under part of the toes.

drop-ins: visiting dancers or occasional class participants. Most big cities have studios offering drop-in classes at various levels. While large professional training schools are mainly for full-time students selected by audition, some also offer a more flexible, less intensive stream with open classes.

en pointe: standing on one's toes in pointe shoes (*see also* pointe shoes).

fouetté: a whipping movement. May be a short whipped movement of the raised foot or the sharp whipping around of the body from one direction to another. There are a variety of supported (with a partner) and unsupported fouetté turns.

gel toepads: gel-filled, cup-shaped protective lining to ease the pressure of pointe shoes against toes and bunions. Some dancers use toepads made of synthetic foam or wads of lambs' wool; stoics do without padding in the belief it will toughen their feet in the long run.

Grand Pas Classique: a technically taxing showpiece pas de deux with music by Gsovsky/Auber.

matrioshka doll: a set of brightly colored hollow wooden dolls of varying sizes, designed to fit inside each other. The traditional type often depicts a span of generations ranging from great-grandmother to baby girl, but modern dolls intended for tourists feature anything from football teams to politicians.

pas de deux: a dance for two; usually refers to a ballet's leading male and female "characters" performing together.

patronymic: a name derived from that of the father or a paternal ancestor.

pirouette: whirl or spin. A complete turn of the body on one foot, on pointe or demi-pointe. Pirouettes are performed turning inward toward the supporting leg or outward in the direction of the raised leg, with the body well centered over the supporting leg and the hips and shoulders aligned.

pointe shoes: satin ballet slippers worn by dancers when dancing on pointe. The toes of pointe shoes are reinforced with several layers of strong glue or lacquer in between layers of material.

repertoire teachers: usually dancers or former dancers, such teachers specialize in interpretive technique and coaching students in standard ballet repertoire. They are often brought in as guest teachers to stage ballets or excerpts.

seconde, à la: to the second position; a pose on one leg with the other one extended to the side either 45°, 90°, 120°, or 180° off the floor.

Shchedrin's adaptation: Russian composer Rodion Shchedrin reset Bizet's original score for *Carmen,* emphasizing strings and percussion, whereas Bizet's original score relied heavily on the woodwinds.

Slavonic: related to the Slavic languages, including Russian.

soft blocks: pointe shoes recycled as soft shoes by crushing the tips and removing the shank.

turn-out: the ability of the dancer to turn his or her feet and legs out from the hip joints to a 90-degree position.

Vaganova: Russian ballet technique introduced by Agrippina Vaganova and characterized by generous, lyrical movement flowing from the heart and torso. A former dancer of the Maryinsky Theatre (later known as the Kirov Ballet), Vaganova began teaching in 1918 and was appointed director of the state ballet school in St. Petersburg (then Leningrad) in 1935. Vaganova's method has become the classic method of the entire Soviet choreographic school.

W5: a CTV news program specializing in investigative journalism. The theme for the eight-minute clip on our Moscow adventure was, "Would you let your teenage daughters…?"

Wili: from the ballet *Giselle,* the vampire-like maidens who died before their wedding days and danced passionately beyond the grave.

About the Author

At fourteen, Olympia Dowd was offered a job as a soloist with the Moscow City Ballet. She toured with the Ballet company for a year, traveling through Asia and Europe. Today, she lives in Vancouver and continues to pursue a career in dance.